P9-CQQ-450

P9-CQQ-450

The HIGHEST TRIBUTE

Thurgood Marshall's Life, Leadership, and Legacy

Written by

Kekla Magoon

Illustrated by

Laura Freeman

Quill Tree Books
An Imprint of HarperCollinsPublishers

For Cynthia
—K.M.

For Griffin
—L.F.

Quill Tree Books is an imprint of HarperCollins Publishers.

The Highest Tribute: Thurgood Marshall's Life, Leadership, and Legacy
Text copyright © 2021 by Kekla Magoon
Illustrations copyright © 2021 by Laura Freeman
All rights reserved. Manufactured in Italy.
No part of this book may be used or reproduced in any manner whatsoever without
written permission except in the case of brief quotations embodied in critical articles
and reviews. For information address HarperCollins Children's Books,
a division of HarperCollins Publishers, 195 Broadway, New York, NY 10007.
www.harpercollinschildrens.com

ISBN 978-0-06-291251-0

The artist used Photoshop to create the digital illustrations for this book.
Typography by Rachel Zegar
20   21   22   23   24   RTLO   10   9   8   7   6   5   4   3   2   1
❖
First Edition

"In recognizing the humanity of our fellow beings,
we pay ourselves the highest tribute."
—Thurgood Marshall

Thoroughgood Marshall was in second grade when he decided that if there was something he didn't like about the world, he should try to change it. He started with his own name. *Thurgood,* he decided. *From now on, I will be known as Thurgood Marshall.*

WHITES
ONLY

DRINKIN

WHITE

WHITES ONLY
MAIDS IN UNIFORM ACCEPTED

There were many more things Thurgood wanted to change about his world.

He grew up in Baltimore, Maryland—a segregated city. The law required Black people and white people to use separate public facilities, such as restrooms and water fountains. Many stores and restaurants had "Whites Only" signs. Theaters had separate seating areas, too. Thurgood observed big differences between the spaces for Black people and white people. They were separate but they were not equal. It was wrong. But it was the law, and one little Black boy couldn't change it. Could he?

Around the dinner table, Thurgood's father led discussions about important issues like segregation. His parents were determined to see their children break the boundaries the country's laws had set for them.

If Thurgood was going to change anything, he had a lot of work ahead of him. But sometimes it was hard for him to believe it was worth trying.

Thurgood's parents expected him to do well in school, but goofing around was much more fun. Sometimes he got in big trouble for misbehaving in class. One teacher assigned him to read the Constitution of the United States as punishment. The plan backfired. Thurgood loved learning about the law!

The nation's Constitution says all people are equal, so how can segregation laws treat people differently? Thurgood wondered.

Thurgood joined the high school debate club. It was a good place to ask his questions and discuss solutions. He liked discovering facts that he could use to win an argument. He liked being part of a team. He liked using words and ideas to persuade people to see complicated issues in a new way.

Lincoln University

Segregation meant Thurgood had to attend a
Black college, so he went to Lincoln University
in Pennsylvania. First things first: He joined
the debate team. Later, he met Vivian "Buster"
Burey, who would soon become his wife. Buster
encouraged Thurgood's dreams.

Thurgood would become the first to do a lot of things that a Black person had never done before. In the past, debate teams from Black colleges only debated other Black teams. Thurgood's team knew this was wrong. Could they change it? They could! In 1928, the Lincoln University debate team faced Pennsylvania State College in the first interracial debate between U.S. colleges.

Thurgood wanted to become a lawyer, but his preferred school, the University of Maryland, did not admit Black students. This was wrong. But it was the law, and he couldn't change it . . . yet. Thurgood went to Howard University Law School in Washington, DC, another Black college. Professor Charles Hamilton Houston shared Thurgood's belief that determined, educated people could do what was necessary to change unfair laws. Once again, Thurgood became part of a team using words and ideas to affect the world.

Thurgood studied harder than ever and graduated first in his class. As a young lawyer in Baltimore, he represented Donald Murray, a Black man who wanted to attend the University of Maryland. The school's whites-only admission policy was wrong, and it was time to try to change it. Thurgood won the case, resulting in the nation's first court order to desegregate a school. This accomplishment was one step in a long-term plan to urge the courts to outlaw segregation everywhere.

Thurgood gained a reputation for being an excellent attorney. He took on civil rights cases all across the country. He worked alongside Professor Houston, who became special counsel to the National Association for the Advancement of Colored People (NAACP) in New York. When Professor Houston retired, Thurgood took over his role as the lead attorney in the team of activists.

Thurgood's most famous case was the pinnacle of his fight against school segregation. Black families in Topeka, Kansas, wanted the board of education to allow their Black children to attend the all-white school. The local court in Kansas said this was illegal. Thurgood appealed the decision to the United States Supreme Court, the highest court in the country. He presented his evidence, and in 1954, the court decided: school segregation was unconstitutional. Thurgood had won the case!

This victory rocked the nation. The nine Supreme Court justices made decisions that affected the law throughout the country. The case may have started in Kansas, but the decision would apply to schoolchildren in every U.S. state.

Thurgood argued and won seven important cases before the Supreme Court.

Each case was one piece of his plan to make the United States a fair and equal place for all people. His colleagues nicknamed him "Mr. Civil Rights."

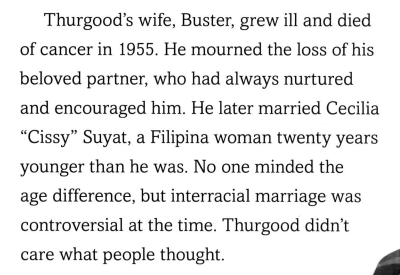

Thurgood's wife, Buster, grew ill and died of cancer in 1955. He mourned the loss of his beloved partner, who had always nurtured and encouraged him. He later married Cecilia "Cissy" Suyat, a Filipina woman twenty years younger than he was. No one minded the age difference, but interracial marriage was controversial at the time. Thurgood didn't care what people thought.

He loved Cissy. They had two children together: Thurgood Jr. and John. His family was another team Thurgood enjoyed being part of. Cissy worked alongside him at the NAACP, and his sons would grow up to take jobs in public service, working for justice in their own ways.

In 1961, President John F. Kennedy asked Thurgood to become a judge. Instead of arguing cases himself, other lawyers would argue cases in front of him and he would get to decide.

Thurgood accepted the job. He listened to over one hundred court cases! None of his decisions was ever overturned by a higher court.

In 1965, President Lyndon Johnson promoted Thurgood to serve as solicitor general. He would argue cases in the Supreme Court again; this time on behalf of the U.S. government. He was the first Black person to hold such a high position.

Thurgood won fourteen more Supreme Court cases! He had argued and won more Supreme Court cases than any other attorney.

Cissy and Thurgood celebrated good news on June 12, 1967, when the Supreme Court struck down the ban on interracial marriage. The wave of change was growing stronger.

The very next day, President Johnson nominated Thurgood Marshall for a seat on the Supreme Court. Many people did not like the idea of a Black Supreme Court justice. Thurgood had to appear before Congress for hearings. They asked him hard questions about the law to try to trick him. But after years of being a lawyer, Thurgood was used to facing pressure from powerful people. He stayed calm, and when he was finished speaking, Congress could not deny that he was qualified.

Thurgood Marshall was sworn in to the United States Supreme Court on October 2, 1967. He was no longer a young Black boy from Baltimore, limited by unjust laws. Now he was one of the people who made sure the laws were fair.

As the first Black member of the Supreme Court, Justice Marshall stood up for civil rights in the same way he did as an attorney.

Among the nine justices, decisions were made not by one person but by the group. All those years on his school debate teams and as part of a team of civil rights attorneys helped prepare Thurgood for the challenge of Supreme Court deliberations. Thurgood's ideas could not win every argument, but he was good at making his opinion heard. If he knew a law was wrong, he was in a stronger position than ever to help change it. Finally, something was right: Thurgood's presence on the court helped change his country's laws forever.

Upon his retirement, Thurgood left all his private writings, notes, and journals to the Library of Congress for immediate public use, breaking the tradition of Supreme Court papers staying sealed for fifty years. If his ideas could continue to help create equality, he wanted them to be seen—by scholars, law students, or anyone with a desire to peek behind the scenes of history.

MARK T. MOORE, PRESIDENT

O. G. F. DUNCAN, VICE-PRESIDENT
HIME

FRANK C. BURTS, VICE-PRESIDENT
110 E. LAKE AVE., TAMPA

C. BEATRICE McLIN, SECRETARY
335 JACKSON ST., N., ST. PETERSBURG

EMMA A. PICKETT, ASSISTANT SECRETARY
81 N. BRYAN ST., ORLANDO

REV. K. S. JOHNSON, TREASURER
601 CYPRESS AVE., SANFORD

BOARD OF DIRECTORS

BOYNTON BEACH
SUSIE P. WADE

BREVARD COUNTY
ELMER SILAS

FT. PIERCE
REV. J. W. WILLIAMS

JACKSONVILLE
C. M. VAUGHT

LAKE WALES
W. H. P.

FLORIDA STATE CONFERENCE OF THE

National Association
FOR THE
Advancement of Colored People

Mims, Fla.
June 30, 1944

Attorney Thurgood
Special Coun
69 Fifth
New

Supreme Court of the United States
Washington, D. C. 20543

JUSTICE THURGOOD MARSHALL

Re: No. 76-811, Regents of the

MEMORANDUM TO THE

I repeat, for ne

this case depends on

Regents as admitting

Mr. Chief Justice, May

We appear as am

believe that they prese

questions regarding

by indirect means

When he died at age eighty-four, Thurgood Marshall was laid in state in the Supreme Court rotunda, an honor given to only one other justice before him. The whole country knew and still knows: through his lifetime of service to humanity, Thurgood Marshall earned himself the highest tribute.

THURGOOD MARSHALL TIMELINE

July 2, 1908

Thoroughgood Marshall is born in Baltimore, Maryland

June 24, 1925

Thurgood graduates from Frederick Douglass High School

September 1925

He starts college at Lincoln University in Pennsylvania

September 4, 1929

He marries Vivian "Buster" Burey

June 1930

Thurgood graduates cum laude from Lincoln University

Fall 1930

He starts law school at Howard University

June 1933

He graduates magna cum laude from Howard University Law School

October 11, 1933

Upon passing the bar exam, Thurgood signs the Maryland "test book" and officially becomes "attorney at law"

November 1933

He begins a private law practice in Baltimore

January 1934

He begins work with the NAACP in Baltimore, taking cases on referral

June 21, 1935

A Maryland judge rules in *Murray v. Pearson*, desegregating the University of Maryland law school

December 1935

He becomes the lead attorney for the Baltimore NAACP

October 1936

Thurgood and Buster move to New York City, where he works as assistant special counsel to Charles Hamilton Houston of the NAACP, eventually succeeding him as special counsel

February 12, 1940
He wins his first case in the U.S. Supreme Court, *Chambers v. Florida*

December 9, 1952
Thurgood argues *Brown v. Board of Education* in front of the Supreme Court

December 8, 1953
He re-argues *Brown v. Board of Education* in the Supreme Court

May 17, 1954
The Supreme Court rules on *Brown v. Board of Education,* declaring segregation unconstitutional

February 1955
Thurgood's wife, Vivian "Buster" Burey, dies from cancer

December 1955
Thurgood and Cecilia Suyat marry

August 12, 1956
Their son Thurgood Marshall Jr. is born

July 6, 1958
Their son John Marshall is born

October 5, 1961
Nominated by President Kennedy, Thurgood becomes a judge on the United States Court of Appeals for the Second Circuit

August 23, 1965
Appointed by President Johnson, Thurgood becomes U.S. solicitor general

June 13, 1967
President Johnson nominates Thurgood for associate justice of the U.S. Supreme Court

July 15–24, 1967
Thurgood participates in Congressional Confirmation Hearings

September 1, 1967
Thurgood becomes the first Black justice of the U.S. Supreme Court

October 1, 1991
Thurgood retires after twenty-four years of service on the court

January 24, 1993
Thurgood dies of heart failure in Bethesda, Maryland, at age eighty-four

MAJOR COURT CASES

Thurgood's work had a huge impact on United States law. As an attorney, he argued more cases in front of the U.S. Supreme Court than any other lawyer before him. As solicitor general and then associate justice, he participated in landmark rulings, too. These are a few of the many important cases he participated in:

Murray v. Pearson (1935):

In Thurgood's first big case as an attorney, he represented Donald Murray, a young Black man who wanted to attend the University of Maryland Law School. At the time, the school did not admit Black students. On June 21, 1935, a judge ruled that the school's policy was not equal. Thurgood won the case again in the Maryland Court of Appeals on January 15, 1936, which resulted in the first court order to desegregate a school in the United States.

Chambers v. State of Florida (1940):

This was the first case Thurgood argued before the Supreme Court. In 1933, four young Black men were accused of murder in Florida. They were arrested, held in jail for a week, aggressively questioned, and denied access to attorneys. The men at first insisted they were innocent, but after many days of this cruel treatment, they confessed and were convicted. Thurgood helped appeal their case to higher courts. On February 12, 1940, the U.S. Supreme Court found that the men's confessions had been forced by police and should not count. The majority ruling determined that police officers, lawyers, and judges must use due process of law, which means they must treat people fairly and follow the rules when they suspect someone has committed a crime.

Sweatt v. Painter (1950):

Thurgood represented Heman Marion Sweatt, who wanted to attend the all-white University of Texas Law School. The school had attempted to create a separate program for Black law students, but Thurgood and the NAACP argued that such segregation would not offer a truly equal education. Thurgood earned a unanimous decision in his favor from the U.S. Supreme Court on June 5, 1950. This case was one of several that paved the way for school integration to take effect nationwide.

Brown v. Board of Education of Topeka (1954):

Oliver Brown, on behalf of his daughter, Linda, joined with other Black families in Topeka, Kansas, to sue the board of education. Thurgood argued the case before the U.S. Supreme Court twice, once in December 1952 and again in December 1953. On May 17, 1954, a unanimous Supreme Court ruling declared school segregation unconstitutional, because separate education facilities were inherently unequal.

Browder v. Gayle (1956):

Thurgood and other NAACP attorneys represented Aurelia Browder and several other women who had experienced discrimination on the Montgomery, Alabama, bus system. The group sued W. A. Gayle, the mayor of Montgomery, in federal court. On June 5, 1956, three judges on the U.S. District Court ruled (2–1) that segregated buses were unconstitutional because the Fourteenth Amendment gives all citizens the right to equal treatment under the law. The U.S. Supreme Court affirmed the decision on November 13, 1956. The Montgomery bus system was integrated on December 20, 1956.

Miranda v. State of Arizona (1966):

Ernesto Miranda was arrested, charged with a crime, and questioned by police. He answered questions and signed a confession because he did not know he had the right to stay quiet or ask for an attorney to help him, and no one told him. Miranda's attorney argued that the confession should not count because Miranda had not understood that the questions he answered for police could be used against him in court.

The Miranda case came to Thurgood while he was solicitor general. He argued the case for the government before the Supreme Court and lost. On June 13, 1966, the justices ruled (5–4) in favor of Miranda. Because of this ruling, police officers must now inform people of their right to remain silent and their right to an attorney when they are being arrested or questioned.

As associate justice, Thurgood heard and ruled (or dissented) in many influential cases, too. He was on the bench when the judges ruled in:

Roe v. Wade (1973), which determined that state laws restricting access to abortion violated the right to privacy between doctor and patient.

United States v. Nixon (1974), which determined that the president of the United States is not above the law, cannot withhold evidence, and remains subject to criminal prosecution.

Regents of the University of California v. Bakke (1978), which upheld affirmative action as a legal means for schools to promote diversity.

FURTHER READING

Thurgood, by Jonah Winter, illustrated by Bryan Collier (Schwartz & Wade Books, 2019).

A Picture Book of Thurgood Marshall, by David Adler, illustrated by Robert Casilla (Holiday House, 1997).

Through My Eyes, by Ruby Bridges (Scholastic Press, 1999).

I Dissent: Ruth Bader Ginsburg Makes Her Mark, by Debbie Levy, illustrated by Elizabeth Baddeley (Simon & Schuster, 2016).

Turning Pages: My Life Story, by Sonia Sotomayor (Philomel Books, 2018).

BIBLIOGRAPHY

Gibson, Larry S. Young Thurgood: The Making of a Supreme Court Justice. Amherst, NY: Prometheus Books, 2012.

Haygood, Wil. Showdown: Thurgood Marshall and the Supreme Court Nomination that Changed America. New York: Vintage Books, 2015.

James, Rawn, Jr. Root and Branch: Charles Hamilton Houston, Thurgood Marshall, and the Struggle to End Segregation. New York: Bloomsbury, 2010.

King, Gilbert. Devil in the Grove: Thurgood Marshall, the Groveland Boys and the Dawn of a New America. New York: Harper Perennial, 2012.

Time Special Edition. Thurgood Marshall: The Visionary. Time, July 24, 2018.